Chameleons in Captivity

by Connie Dorval

Professional Breeders Series®

ISBN 978-0-9767334-3-9

Copies available from:

ECO Herpetological Publishing & Distribution
915 Seymour Ave. Lansing, MI 48906 USA
telephone: 517.487.5595 fax: 517.371.2709
email: ecoorders@hotmail.com website: http://www.reptileshirts.com

T-Rex Products, Inc.
http://t-rexproducts.com

Zoo Book Sales
http://www.zoobooksales.com

LIVINGART publishing
http://www.livingartpublishing.com

Design and layout by Russ Gurley.
Cover design by Rafael Porrata.
Printed in China

Front Cover: A beautiful and wary adult male Panther Chameleon. Photo by Michael Monge.
Back Cover: A handsome adult male Veiled Chameleon. Photo by Bill Love.

ACKNOWLEDGEMENTS

Dedicated to my parents for so much loving support and to Millie and Puff who started my passion, taught me and blessed me.

Heartfelt appreciation to all of you who have helped and supported my journey in this field. There are so many of you!

A special thank you to my husband, Antonio Varrasso, my best friend and cheerleader! Also to those who have integrally contributed to what I do – the Chameleon Information Network, Brian Potter, Diane Rooke-Harris, Linda Horgan, Dr. Wolfgang Zenker, Susan Berezuk, David Souliere, Tricia Gelinas, Scotty Allen and Nicole Donelle, - and of course, a wink to Bayard, Rob and Grant. I love you guys and you know why!

I need also to thank Jon Coote and T-Rex for their consistent interest in advancement and improvement toward reptiles and their husbandry. Jon is ever pursuing for my views as a breeder and the ambition to provide better for T-Rex. I applaud their effort to recognize and support the very different needs of each reptile family, especially chameleons.

A big thank you to those who supplied wonderful photos contained in this book, including Tyler Stewart, Michael Monge, Russ Gurley, Kevin McCurley, Bob Ashley, VI Pets, and of course Bill Love. Your help is much appreciated.

Last, but not least, my warmest appreciation to Bob and Sheri Ashley for their professional support and friendship over the years and the opportunity to give my journey a voice.

Thank you!

Contents

INTRODUCTION

Photo by Michael Monge.

Chameleons are in a unique class of their own and for anyone keeping these exotic dragons of herpetoculture, if it is not acknowledged from the onset, this fact will be swiftly discovered. Beyond their unusual physicality and their curious nature, a chameleon in captivity has specific husbandry needs that require diligence and understanding for long-term success and a natural lifespan. Their needs aren't difficult, but they are very necessary. Chameleons will not thrive long with improper husbandry. Of course, knowledge is the key. With every keeper out there, a new variation on a theory is out there. Many theories work, some don't. This book is meant to discuss information that has worked very successfully in terms of keeping and breeding chameleons in captivity for several years by the author.

Long considered mysterious creatures, over the years many theories in regard to chameleons have developed with some proved and some disproved. The most famous of course, is that chameleons change color to match what they are perched on or near. As much as they themselves would love it to be so, it is not. Chameleons enhance, darken and fade their coloration, while only some species completely adopt full change of color. For any of these variations, the change in coloration is a reflection of thermoregulation or communication. Of course camouflage must still be addressed. While chameleons do not adopt coloration for the purpose of camouflage, their natural species body design and coloration are designed for a life dependant on the art of blending into the environment.

In terms of theories, another common one to be addressed is the thought that a female chameleon will die at sexual maturity if not bred. This simply is not true. If a female dies at this term of life, it has everything to do with husbandry and/or the overall health of that particular animal. A healthy female chameleon will pass infertile eggs without concern. However, it is the responsibility of the keeper to watch for the signs of egg laying and to provide a suitable site when necessary.

Chapter ONE: CHAMELEONS IN NATURE

While most chameleon species are found in Africa and the surrounding islands, particularly Madagascar, some species can also be found in southern Europe (Spain, Portugal and Greece), some neighboring Mediterranean islands and the East (Saudi Arabia, India and Sri Lanka). Of the approximately 160 species of chameleon (and approximately 190 subspecies) most live in forests or on the edges of heavy vegetation, with a few species inhabiting desert climates.

A cryptic Panther Chameleon in the dappled sunlight of its habitat in Madagascar. Photo by Bill Love.

In fact, chameleon habitat can vary depending on species. These diverse sites include wooded forests, grasslands, montane rainforests and shrubby savannas. While all chameleon species appear morphologically adapted to the arboreal lifestyle and most are, there are a few exceptions that have taken to ground level, species such as *Chamaeleo namaquensis* and some species of *Brookesia* and *Rhampholeon*.

Chapter TWO: CHAMELEON BIOLOGY

Most chameleons such as this beautiful blue Panther Chameleon are excellent climbers. Photo by Tyler Stewart.

There is little doubt that the anatomical features of these unusual creatures, many of which appear exclusive only to chameleons, are fascinating. Of course, their most famous feature is their mastery of camouflage. Beyond that, there is a host of other interesting abilities or features chameleons utilize as who they are and how they survive. Aspects such as a shooting tongue that extends the length of their bodies to catch prey, binocular eyes that move in two different directions and allow the chameleon to see behind and in front at the same time, the ability to drop from tree tops unharmed or a prehensile tail that can catch a branch half down and stop the animal mid-air.

The classification of the chameleon can be complicated and a matter of debate among even the most educated of reptilian enthusiasts. However, the family tree for chameleons seems to be accepted as follows: class of Reptilia, order of Squamata, suborder of Lizards (Sauria), family of Chamaeleonidae. Then there are two subfamilies

Head scalation of a male Panther Chameleon from Ambanja, Madagascar. Photo by Bill Love.

of chameleon being Chamaeleonidae (typical) and Brookesiinae (atypical). The subfamily of Chamaeleonidae includes the Genera of Bradypodion, Calumma, Chamaeleo and Furcifer. The subfamily of Brookesinae includes the chameleons often referred to as pygmies, the Genera of Brookesia and Rhampholeon.

The subfamilies of Chamaeleonidae include the most commonly kept chameleons in captivity – species such as *C. calyptratus*, *F. pardalis,* and *C. jacksonii*. The members of this subfamily are most typically notable for their prehensile tail and their agility of movement and color compared to their smaller, less active and drab cousins.

Chameleon anatomy is designed to avoid predation while giving the chameleon apt predatory skill in their hunt for food. They are meant not only to be masters at camouflage, but masters at ambush as well.

The first physical aspect that should be discussed is the chameleon's amazing coloration and how it works to blend with its environment and communicate to others of the same species at the same time. While it is not true that chameleons can change to any color to match their environment, chameleons do display dramatic coloration reflective of their specific habitat and locale. They can also change or

Male Panther Chameleons are without a doubt some of the most beautiful reptiles on the planet. Photo by Michael Monge.

brighten their individual coloration as a communication to others reflecting mood and intention. For example when two males meet, their agitation and aggression are displayed with an intense brightening of color, coupled with a physical display of intent. A gravid female will use coloration to dissuade a courting male.

Communication is not the only purpose behind their color change. Chameleon skin is thermal sensitive. At rest or when the temperatures rise, chameleons tend to be pale. When a chameleon is cold, it will darken to attract the heat.

As a chameleon grows, it will periodically shed its skin. Younger chameleons will shed more often naturally as they are growing rapidly. The skin will become white and begin to break off in patches. At this time, the chameleon may be seen rubbing itself along available objects like leaves and branches and stretching often, all in aid to remove the shedding skin. This process can last from a few hours to a few days. The shed should be complete. If old patches of skin remain and the shed is incomplete, it can be an indicator that the humidity levels are incorrect for the species, or perhaps it can be a sign of an ailing chameleon in some way. If this occurs, the overall health and well being of the chameleon should be observed.

A beautiful orange male Panther Chameleon. Photo by Tyler Stewart.

Posture change can also be a form of communication or camouflage. Chameleons will shiver or wobble in an effort to imitate a leaf moving in the breeze and avoid detection. They will flatten or narrow to imitate their surroundings and assume cover, and they are capable of inflating as well, to appear more menacing when the camouflage doesn't work.

Chameleons also have cartilaginous ribs that allow for harmless falls from high heights. In an extreme effort to avoid attack or detection, they will simply drop from where ever they may be perched, and land safely. Neonates are often inclined to display this behavior readily.

Paramount to chameleon survival is their acute vision. Since they virtually lack any sense of smell or hearing, a chameleon is very dependant on sight. In fact, right from their first view of the world, chameleons have a keen sense of vision and recognition. Neonates

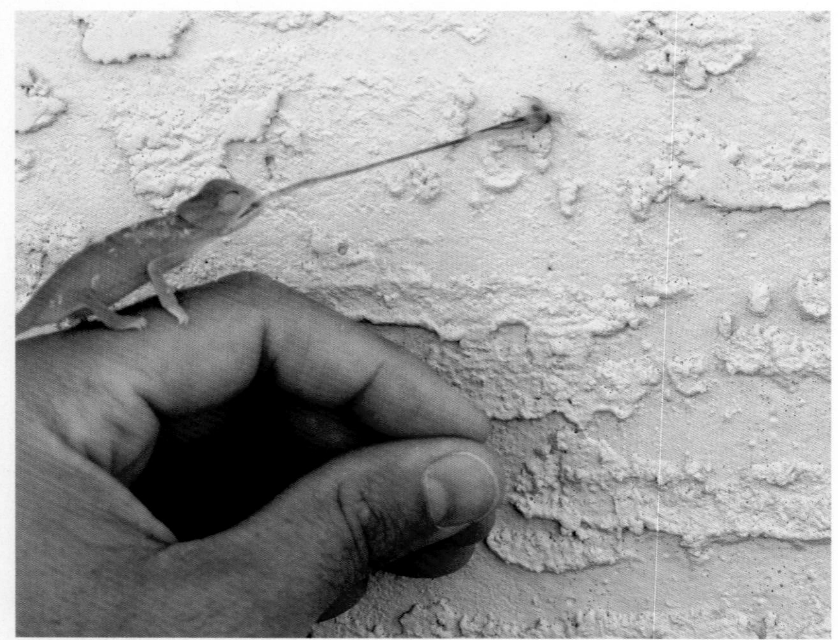

The long tongue of chameleons is one of their most amazing characteristics. Photo by Michael Monge.

react incredibly quickly to potential danger and will always spot you before you do them. Their eye movement range encompasses 90 degrees vertically and 180 degrees horizontally.

A chameleon's tongue is another interesting and unique aspect to be discussed. At approximately one and a half times their body length, a chameleon catches prey by shooting its tongue at the target and the prey is captured by the sticky grip of its bulbous tip. A chameleon will then chew its food and swallow.

The tongue also seems to be used to detect chemical messages. While not fully understood, it seems that chameleons do noticeably mark branches by rubbing their cloaca along a branch and chameleons are often observed tasting their surroundings with the tip of their tongue.

Designed for life in the branches, chameleons have five toes fused in opposing groups on each foot, with the front having two toes fused together on the outside and three on the inside, and the reverse for the back feet. All toes have claws.

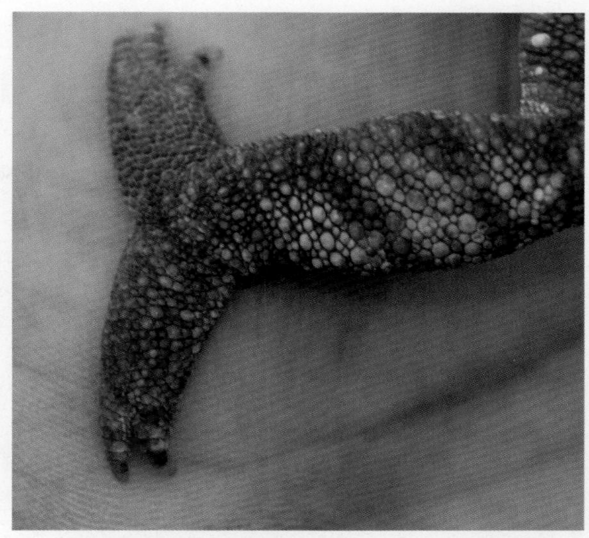

The fused toes of chameleons help them grip branches tightly as they climb. Photo by Bob Ashley.

Along with feet made for arboreal locomotion, chameleons have strongly prehensile tails that aid greatly in balance and climbing. Species that inhabit the higher canopy levels have longer tails. Likewise, chameleons inhabiting the lower ranges have shorter tails.

Chameleons cannot hear sound as we do. They do not possess ears per se. Chameleons instead have an auditory area that registers vibration. Upon chameleon observation, you will notice that they are not vocal creatures. Instead, when they do attempt to make noise, its either a vibrating hum or a hiss, and usually only used as a warning.

Chapter THREE: CHOOSING A CHAMELEON

Captive-hatched (or captive born) chameleons are always the best choice. This is a female Jackson's chameleon and her newborn baby. Photo by Michael Monge.

Certainly if you are considering owning a chameleon, there are several factors to consider. Chameleons are often viewed as 'high maintenance' in relation to other reptiles in captivity. It's not that chameleons are difficult really. It's that they have specific needs that can differ entirely from other reptile species, but as long as you understand what your chameleon will need and you adhere to that, the difficulty diminishes.

Some important aspects to understand, particularly if you are looking to simply keep a chameleon as a pet, would be:

Choose captive-bred over wild caught import chameleons. Unless you are considered an experienced chameleon keeper and have

Healthy chameleons will readily feed on a range of insect prey. Photo by Tyler Stewart.

access to good veterinary service, a captive-bred chameleon is the best choice. Import chameleons often arrive heavily parasitized, dehydrated and starved and can be difficult to acclimate without experience.

Most chameleon species (with perhaps few exceptions) are always best kept singly. Chameleons are not social animals and actually prefer a solitary environment, which includes males and females even more so. The only time pairs are found together is during a brief mating courtship otherwise chameleons are territorial animals that prefer life on their own.

Female egg laying species will need to occasionally lay eggs, regardless of being exposed to a male. When choosing a pet, this needs to be considered. It isn't difficult to provide an egg-laying site, but will be necessary if you have a female in your care. A healthy female chameleon will lay infertile eggs once or twice a year without difficulty if she's healthy.

A healthy juvenile Panther Chameleon. Photo by Bill Love.

When it comes to choosing a specific chameleon to take home you will want to pay close attention to some particular aspects.

First be sure that the chameleon is active. Chameleons are diurnal which means they are alert and moving during daylight hours. A sleeping chameleon during the day is often a sign of illness or stress.

You will also want to be sure that the chameleon appears to have good body weight and is eating and drinking. This is easily assessed by looking at the eyes, head pads and tail. Healthy chameleons do not have sunken eye turrets, sunken head pads on the top of their heads and the tailbone should not be exceptionally apparent.

Another excellent indicator is the area around the cloaca and fecal consistency. Healthy chameleons should not have fecal smearing around their cloaca and the fecal itself should not be runny or filled with mucous or blood. This can be an indicator of a parasitic or bacterial infection.

Be sure that a chameleon you may wish to purchase is not breathing from its mouth, wheezing or has any form of mucous or discharge around its mouth, nasal passage or eyes. This can be a sign of respiratory infection.

Check chameleons for any swellings or deformities when considering a purchase. Photo by Bob Ashley.

Lastly, avoid chameleons with unusual swellings or deformities that may also indicate a health issue. Even captive chameleons can suffer from nutritional deficiencies that can create visible problems. A healthy chameleon will walk with a tight grip, upright, alert and agile.

Chapter FOUR: HOUSING

A row of screen cages for housing multiple chameleons. Photo by Tyler Stewart.

When it comes to housing and maintenance, it is impossible to create a standard for chameleons in general. With so many species inhabiting so many different regions, habitats and elevations, each species must be further researched in order for you as the keeper to understand the natural environment of your specific chameleon. More than any other reptile in captivity, chameleons do need a home designed close to their own natural environment in terms of temperature and humidity. However, as long as you understand the species specifics of your chameleon, there certainly are general guidelines and considerations.

Indoor Caging

The idea to keeping a chameleon in captivity is to try to provide an environment indoors similar to their natural environment outdoors, or at least as close as possible. The truth is, indoor chameleon maintenance is never as suitable as their outdoor habitat. However, with the

This arboreal Vision cage has been established for a young chameleon. Photo by Bob Ashley.

growing knowledge of chameleon husbandry and the subsequent growth of the supply industry, keeping chameleons as pets has become more successful than ever.

The first consideration is the cage itself. The type of cage has been a source of some debate over the years. Generally most breeders will tell you that fully screened enclosures are the absolute choice for keeping chameleons in captivity. While I do personally adhere and advise it, I feel I should divulge fairly that for several years as a breeder starting out, I did use glass enclosures with a screen top and managed to do so very successfully with the species *C. calyptratus* and *F. pardalis*. It wasn't until I began to work with more species that I switched my entire facility over to fully screened enclosures. However, I will note here that I believe those are the only two species of chameleon that will tolerate enclosed caging long term and it is vital that the keeper regularly wash and disinfect this type of enclosure. Glass tanks will become a perfect breeding ground for bacteria in short order.

Therefore, while there are suitable compromises that do work for some, certainly screened or mostly screened enclosures seem to be the most adequate caging type for captive chameleons. Arboreal style enclosures that are higher vertically are naturally more suited to chameleon lifestyle, however most species will also adapt to a horizontal style enclosure.

Size is also another important consideration. Since each species and sex of chameleon varies greatly, it is essential to know the full adult size of the chameleon you intend to house and build or purchase a cage accordingly. The general rule of thumb is that the cage should be three times the full length of the chameleon in height, width and depth or larger. Larger is always better. Chameleons benefit greatly from a sense of freedom.

The cage décor should consist of several branches with an abundance of foliage that will allow the chameleon plenty of walking options with full coverage to alleviate stress. In my personal opinion, I prefer and recommend fake plants, particularly for a novice chameleon keeper. While real plants are certainly more natural, they can also add to health problems if not chosen and maintained appropriately. First, a real plant must be free of insecticides and non-toxic, as certain species of chameleon will bite on leaves. The soil must be free of perlite and vermiculite since some chameleons for unknown reason will ingest these materials, and once they do it is fatal. Finally, the primary reason I do not favor the use of live foliage in chameleon enclosures is the high potential of gathering and reproducing harmful gram-negative bacterial loads that eventually will create a serious health problem for your chameleon if not maintained properly. A live plant will need to have the soil changed on a very regular basis to prevent illness for the chameleon and the sitting area of the plant will need to be disinfected just as regularly. For this reason, I find it far more hygienic to clean artificial foliage.

Substrate

When choosing a substrate, it's important to remember that a chameleon feeds by shooting its tongue. Therefore, care must be taken to use substrates that cannot cause impaction. In fact, this is often a common inadvertent mistake that is fatal to many chameleons and often the keeper never realizes it. It's important to use something that can be kept clean easily and frequently and cannot be readily ingested by the chameleon when it hunts for insects. Plain soil and fine sand are perhaps the only substrates that can be ingested and passed without difficulty. Keep in mind if these are used, they must be changed regularly to prevent disease. Unsuitable substrates often used with ill effects are wood chips, shavings, small pebbles, coconut or peat fiber or coarse reptile sands. Favorable substrates are outdoor artificial carpet, paper towel, large pieces of cork bark, large stones and even newspaper.

In captivity, chameleons require artificial sources of light. These diurnal reptiles need a natural day cycle to stimulate healthy activity. This is accomplished with two sources - a full spectrum and incandescent source.

Very important for chameleons kept indoors is the use of a full spectrum light source. There are many different sources of full spectrum UVB reptile lights available in fluorescent or mercury vapor form. Many keepers are successfully keeping and breeding chameleons under T-Rex's UVB-heat bulbs®. The fluorescent UVB bulbs must be changed every 8 months to maintain adequate spectrum output. Mercury vapor bulbs have twice the life than that of fluorescent bulbs, and therefore do not require rotation as frequently. The full spectrum lighting should be supplied 12 to 14 hours a day and the chameleon must be able to bask within a 10-inch range to the source. It is also important to note that UVB rays do not penetrate plastic or glass adequately and therefore, screening is the only suitable medium that can be used between the source and the chameleon.

An incandescent spot bulb is used as the heat source for your chameleon. The wattage will vary depending on species, size of enclosure and background temperature. Again, it's important to familiarize yourself with where your chameleon is found naturally to understand the highs and lows of what your chameleon needs in terms of temperature.

The incandescent spot bulb should be sufficiently far enough so that it cannot burn the chameleon. It should also be focused on one end of the enclosure only, so that a gradient is provided and the chameleon can regulate its temperature as it sees fit. Typically, the incandescent is provided 6-8 hours daily and less if the area temperature is close to exceeding the high end for the species you are maintaining. Infrared

A dwarf chameleon explores its environment. Photo by Michael Monge.

bulbs and heat rocks are unsuitable sources of heat for chameleons. At night, it is essential that all the lights are out and the enclosure cools down. Most species of chameleon can take a drop at night as low as 60° F without any ill effect. In fact, a drop of at least 10 degrees at night is most beneficial.

Free-range indoor housing deserves to be advocated here. There are those that have the availability to provide this type of living environment indoors for their chameleon and if so, it should be encouraged. However, it's important to keep in mind that chameleons are territorial, so care should be taken when more than one chameleon is present in such an environment.

Most of the same factors for housing apply. Full-spectrum lighting and a spot basking site are both still necessary along with adequate climbing areas.

For years I maintained some chameleons within open vivariums that allowed them to come and go as they pleased within a room. They would bask, feed and drink within the terraria, then leave to wander or rest within surrounding hanging plants. They all lived to ripe old ages for chameleons in captivity with peak health, and I do believe that the psychological effect of this lifestyle was a factor. However, with any free range type of chameleon environment, potential dangers must be eliminated such as other household pets that could cause harm or direct access to hot lights that could cause a burn for some examples.

Outdoor Caging

Last, yet likely the best enclosure for a chameleon, is outdoors with access to unfiltered, natural sunlight. Of course, depending on where you live this really may not be an option. However, if it is, even for a short period, it is the best environment for your chameleon.

Outdoors, exposed to natural sunlight, chameleons only need a minimum of eight hours a week to maintain peak health. In fact, they can even absorb suitable amounts of UVB in shaded areas as well. If this is an option you might like to utilize, you must be aware that some species can handle more sun and heat than others. So once again, knowing the species of chameleon you are housing and their natural habitat is important before you place your chameleon in full sun. It is also equally as important to remember that the chameleon

This is a simple outdoor enclosure for a young chameleon. Photo by Bob Ashley.

will still need a shaded area or gradient in temperature to thermoregulate.

Lastly, if you choose to house your chameleon outdoors, the enclosure absolutely must be screened and ventilated. Any chameleon will quickly go downhill in a glass or closed enclosure outdoors.

Cleanliness

One of the most important aspects to successfully keeping chameleons in captivity is sustaining a healthy immune system. There are a few factors that can compromise this natural internal system. Incorrect husbandry can create low-grade physical stress that over time will degrade the immune system, with aspects such as temperatures that are too high or too low, constant stress and poor cleanliness. Caging maintenance is vital for controlling opportunistic factors such as viral, bacterial or parasitic infestation, which will weaken a chameleon immune system and eventually overwhelm it. Insects, particularly crickets, can be prime introduction hosts for such pathogens, as can feces, water and live plant material. Obviously these factors cannot be eliminated from chameleon husbandry, however measures can and should be taken to maintain low exposure.

At least once or twice weekly, the enclosure and cage furniture should be cleaned and rinsed well of any feces, dead insects and insect feces. Once a month the entire enclosure and furnishings should be disinfected. Preferably a non-toxic disinfect should be used. There are a few available either through the pet trade or from your veterinarian. If you are unsuccessful at obtaining a non-toxic disinfectant, then a dilution of bleach and water can be used to rinse the enclosure and cage furniture, however rinsing all traces of the bleach dilution is vital. It's also recommended to rinse the non-toxic disinfectant residue as well, as the taste on the cage furniture will not appeal to your chameleon.

Watering

Chameleons do not normally drink from standing water. They are naturally attracted to dripping or running forms of water such as dew or rainfall in the wild. Since this is true for chameleons in captivity, the best methods for providing water is by heavy spraying/misting and/or drip systems provided at a minimum of once daily. Dehydration is a common ailment that slowly creates a health issue without the keepers notice until it is often too late. If water can be supplied more than once a day, naturally it's better. However, if water is only supplied daily, it should be administered generously. Chameleons can go surprisingly long without food, but not without water. Hydration is vital to their long-term health.

When providing water via drip system and/or spraying, it is important to be sure that the water is dripping off the screening and leaves. It's this dripping and running effect that will attract the chameleon and entice it to drink if thirsty.

It should also be noted that chameleons seem to prefer tepid or room temperature water.

Waterfalls also need to be discussed here. People often discover that chameleons are naturally attracted to this source for water, however again these are perfect breeding grounds for bacteria. Unless disinfected frequently, they will eventually shorten the lifespan of your chameleon.

A simple drip system that is available from most pet stores. Photo by Bob Ashley.

Misting systems can be added to chameleon enclosures. Photo by Kevin McCurley.

Another factor to be addressed is humidity. For many chameleon species, moderate humidity levels are suitable and can be achieved with the generous spray and/or dripping daily. Some species, specifically montane and pygmy species, require higher humidity levels that may require spraying two to three times daily. This may also be required if you live in a particularly dry area with very low natural humidity levels.

Chapter FIVE: DIET

A Panther Chameleon seconds away from lunch. Photo by Michael Monge.

Diet is another very important aspect to healthy chameleon husbandry and this is particularly so if you intend on breeding in captivity. There are three different aspects that need to be addressed when it comes to chameleon diet: Types of food, gut-loading and supplementation.

What Chameleons Eat

While there are a few species of chameleon that will nibble on vegetation, live insects are the primary to sole source of food. Generally chameleons will eat any live insect that is appropriately sized. However in captivity, while the insects offered should be varied, crickets should be the main staple.

Variety is very important to maintaining good health for your chameleon when it comes to offering insects. Mealworms, super worms,

A Panther Chameleon feeding on the leaves of a *Hibiscus* plant. Photos by Michael Monge.

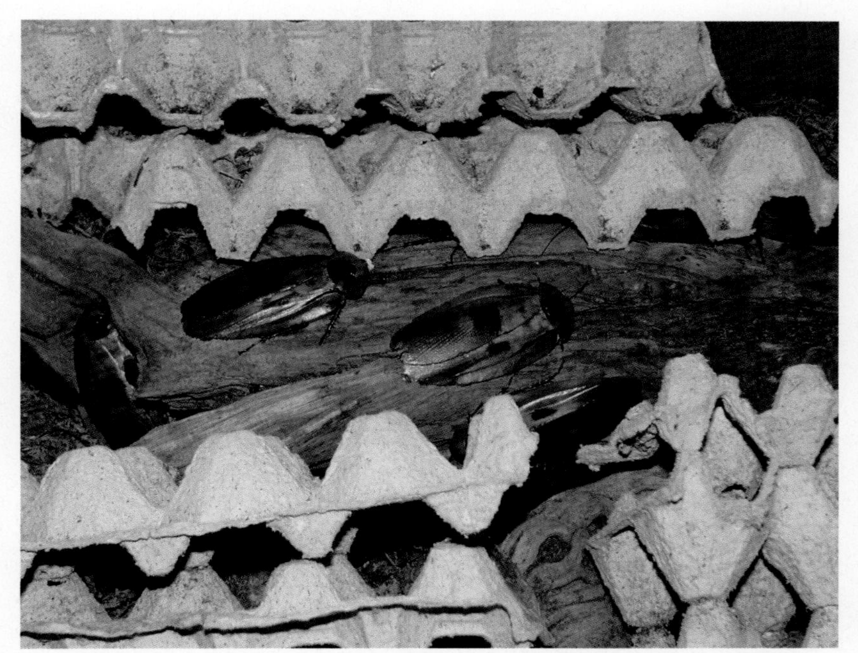
Roaches can be part of the varied diet a keeper offers his or her chameleons. Photo by Russ Gurley.

crickets, wax worms, silk worms, cockroaches, mantids and grasshoppers are all normally eagerly consumed and should be offered regularly. Many of these insects however, while they contain certain nutritional aspects that are healthy in smaller doses, they are often unbalanced and should be offered as part of the varied diet. Ideally, a chameleon should have at least four to five different insects in its diet regularly. Crickets however, seem to be the only commercially available insect that can be used as a main staple, although gut-loading your crickets before feeding is vital.

Insects caught outdoors can be used as food for your chameleon, although you must be certain they have been collected in a pesticide free area.

Gut-loading

This is a term applied to a healthy diet of grains, fruits and vegetables fed to the insects before they are fed to your chameleon. Crickets themselves contain little nutritional value, which is why they are a good main staple to your chameleon diet. They can be readily gut-loaded, while their own nutritional make-up will not interfere with the balance.

Crickets should be fed at least two to three days before being offered as food.

Items to include as part of your insect nutrition are as follows:

Green leafy vegetables (kale, collard, romaine lettuce, mustard greens) fruit (oranges, apples, grapes, papaya, melon) carotene-rich vegetables (carrot, sweet potato, squash) grain mixture base (soybean, wheat, corn, bran, oatmeal) bee pollen rice baby cereal powdered milk commercially available cricket chows

Be sure that fresh food items are offered to the insect's daily and any spoiled or molded items are removed immediately.

Supplementation

This is another area of chameleon husbandry that is often under debate. In fact, it is probably the most controversial aspect to chameleon care to date. As expressed earlier, there are many theories. Some work, some don't.

The prime aspect to keep in mind here is that this is where many health issues begin with chameleons in captivity. Prevention is the key.

When chameleons are kept indoors under artificial UVB their food items must be coated with calcium D_3 supplement without phosphorous. A chameleon needs 2:1 calcium to phosphorous ratio. Insects are naturally higher in phosphorous, therefore calcium needs to be artificially added, but phosphorous does not. T-Rex ICB Cricket Dust® is an excellent supplement for preparing insects for feeding.

The insects should be coated with the supplement before being offered to the chameleon. Females and juveniles should have their insects coated at every feeding, while adult males require a third less, therefore coat the insects four to five days each week. It is also important to use a vitamin supplement once a week in combination with the calcium that is administered more frequently. Personally, I find that natural source vitamins are best offered to the crickets and for the vitamin supplementation, a pre-form source is better to dust the insects fed to your chameleon. Be aware that though some vitamin supplementation is good, a lot is not better. Pre-form vitamins in excess can create more problems. Once a week is sufficient

An adult female Sambava Panther feeding on a superworm. Photo by Tyler Stewart.

Chapter SIX: BREEDING

A mating pair of Panther Chameleons. Photo by Tyler Stewart.

It seems to be a natural progression for many chameleon enthusiasts to desire to produce offspring, and have the experience of incubating and raising young chameleonids. Depending on the species, success can range anywhere from quite simple to difficult. It just seems that some species are easier to incubate and the hatchlings are not difficult, while the opposite can be said for other species. Again, this is an aspect where research needs to be done on your specific species and its natural locale.

Sexing

For each species the sexual dimorphism is different. Typically males are larger than females and more brightly colored. Some males exhibit horns when females do not or not as many (*C. jacksonii*, *C. quadricornis*). Male *C. calyptratus* have a hind spur where the female does not. Some males have an obvious hemipenal swelling (*F. pardalis*, *C. lateralis*).

Reproduction

Mating Panther Chameleons. Photo by Tyler Stewart.

All male chameleon species have their own mating display which can range from a very typical head bobbing for many species, to a brightening or full out change of color, curling of the tail tip back and forth, swaying, a flattening of the body to appear larger and for some, even a low groan or humming. Male *calyptratus* will even ram potential receptive females with their snout.

Normally when a female is exposed to a healthy male, he will begin to display or court the female, usually from a distance at first. If the female indicates receptivity, he will approach. If the female maintains a receptive manner and color, the male will mount her back, slide his cloaca beneath hers and insert the hemipene. Copulation can last from five to twenty minutes typically. Once done, they will separate and depending on the female, they may copulate once or a few times before she resumes a non-receptive pattern and stance.

Females, when first introduced to a male, will either react to the sight of him or not. If they are receptive to the male's advances, their coloration will remain relaxed and unchanged. Often they will even step right into the enclosure and begin walking, which stimulates the

During breeding season, female chameleons often show scarring from the male's sharp claws. Photo by Tyler Stewart.

male to approach. If a female is not receptive, she will rock back and forth, gape, hiss and darken to a non-receptive coloration. If this occurs, the female should be removed and shown back to the male at a later date or it could indicate that she is already gravid if she had been exposed to a male at an earlier date.

Care should be taken not to disturb a copulating pair of chameleons. If they become stressed or agitated at the unwanted audience or movement, the male hemipene can be damaged if the female attempts to leave before he is finished.

Egg Laying And Live Birth

Female chameleons will lay eggs four to eight weeks after copulation for egg laying species. Live bearing species will drop their young any where from three to ten months depending on temperature and species.

Typically for egg laying species, gravid females will stop eating and begin to pace or climb their cage restlessly when ready to lay eggs.

A female Veiled Chameleon digging a hole for deposition of the eggs. Photo by Michael Monge.

At this time, it is essential that the female be provided with a suitable egg-laying site. Often a container within the cage is not considered suitable by many females, unless the cage is very large and can hold the adequate amount of soil while providing solitude and seclusion for the female. While there are some females that will simply deposit eggs in a container of soil or a potted plant within their cage, it is better to provide a larger, secluded area that entices the female to focus on what she needs to do.

A method that works very well for many breeders is a plastic garbage can filled with plain potting soil that is a minimum depth of the length of the female. Suitable lighting should still be provided along with a plant for security and a branch or two for resting and basking. Moisten the soil so that it is damp enough to hold a burrow if you dig into it.

When the gravid female has been placed in her laying site, she should be undisturbed with the exception of watering daily. The entire site should be sprayed generously each day to keep the soil adequately

A female Panther Chameleon laying her eggs. Photo by Tyler Stewart.

ready for the digging female as well as hydration for her.

Once ready, the female will dig often right down to the bottom of the bucket and back in to deposit her eggs. Some females, typically younger, inexperienced females, will dig several tunnels over several days before they decide one is appropriate to deposit the eggs. Care should be taken that the soil does indeed remain moist enough for tunneling throughout this process, so that the tunnel does not collapse on the female, suffocating her.

Many breeders agree that it is psychologically best to allow the female to finish the entire process of burying the eggs once deposited. The female is then returned to her enclosure and the eggs are unburied and moved to an incubating container.

A plastic container with a lid should be used for incubation. Fill it with an inch and a half to two inches of moistened vermiculite (perlite is also suitable), damp enough that if squeezed it does not drip, but will clump when pinched. The eggs are then half buried in the medium usually in rows about a half-inch apart. Finally, three or four one-eighth inch holes are placed in the lid of the container.

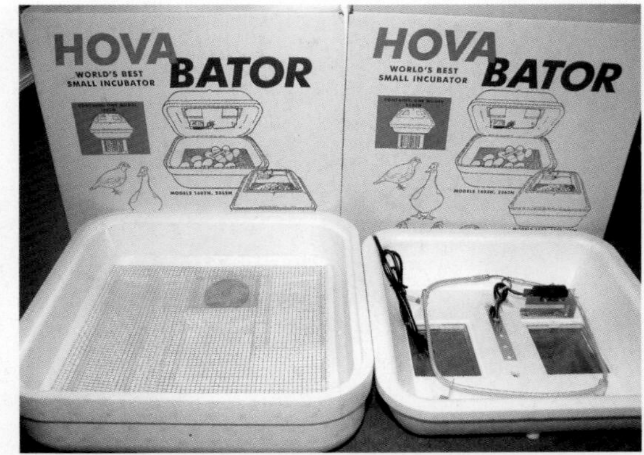

Simple and inexpensive commercial incubators are used by many reptile breeders. Photo by Kevin McCurley.

The moisture consistency should be maintained throughout the incubation period by carefully adding moisture around the outside edge of the eggs if needed. Never allow moisture to drop or spray directly on the incubating eggs as this will fatally suffocate the developing neonate.

A hatchling chameleon emerges from its egg. Photo by Michael Monge.

The hatchling chameleon slices its way out of the egg. Photo by Michael Monge.

The incubation temperature and duration will differ depending on species. However, a typically safe range can be considered 68° F to 74° F for most chameleon species. If the eggs are not fertile, they will mold and discolor within fours weeks typically. Fertile eggs will remain white and turgid, growing slightly as the weeks go by.

Once ready to hatch, the eggs will often, but not always begin to sweat before the egg splits and collapses slightly. The neonate will then absorb the yolk and often remain still, although sometimes with their head polking from the egg, from several hours to a couple of days before walking from the egg. Once the neonate is detached and moving from the egg, it is ready to be moved to an enclosure.

Live bearing females will usually have a girthy appearance, basking frequently and eating less as the time to give birth approaches. Often the birthing process takes place early in the day with most live bearing females, and is a surprise to the keeper. One moment the female is alone in her enclosure and within an hour or two, there can be several small, alert and mobile chameleonids wandering about.

Once ready to give birth, the gravid female will slowly drop the young, one by one as she walks along branches. The young chameleons are enclosed in a thin membrane that is meant to tear away as they fall. Usually the jolt of the drop will stimulate the chameleonid to move and break away from the birthing sack.

At this time, the female should not be disturbed until finished giving birth, and then the young should be removed and housed separately. The female will likely not harm the young within the first initial few hours of birth, however some females will consume some of them eventually if left in the enclosure.

With live bearing species the health of the female, and humidity and heat levels throughout the gravid stage will directly affect the offspring and their chance at survival.

Chapter SEVEN: CARE of YOUNG CHAMELEONS

A one-day old Panther Chameleon watches its surroundings intently. Photo by Tyler Stewart.

It likely could go without mentioning, however, chameleon hatchlings are more delicate than adults and this fact should never be underestimated. While adults can go without food and even adequate moisture for small periods, hatchling chameleonids will go downhill quickly if their care and maintenance is neglected even for a couple of days. Not that this should dissuade from the process. There is nothing as fascinating, endearing and comical as a baby chameleon and the maintenance is worth the experience.

Hatchlings need daily care and can be housed singly or in small groups, depending on the size of the enclosure. Experience has shown that young chameleons grow more rapidly when housed individually, however this is often not a viable option and certainly they can also be housed communally as hatchlings. Typically the rule of thumb should be each neonate needs three times its total body length squared. Therefore the size of enclosure dictates the number of young that can be housed together.

Simple setups for raising young chameleons. Photo by Bob Ashley.

The type of enclosure required follows the same criteria as the adults. However, for substrate it is best to use something simple that cannot be ingested such as paper towel. Another important factor to remember when raising chameleon hatchlings is that one of the most common causes of death in captivity is over-heating. Unlike their parents, the young cannot regulate their body temperatures as adequately and require their keeper to ensure that temperatures are moderate. Often basking bulbs are not even required for the first two months of a hatchlings life in captivity.

Temperatures within mid-to-high seventies during the day is often sufficient for most species as a general rule of thumb, however once again, it is important to know the species you have and the range they inhabit in the wild. Certainly some of the more heat loving hatchling species can tolerate temperatures into the low eighties.

Typically hatchlings will not eat for a day or two after hatching. Food is normally offered on day two sparingly, so that the running insects do not overwhelm them. The hatchlings should also be watered twice daily via a generous misting.

Within the enclosure, it is important to have a lot of full foliage and many branches for the young to feel secure and reduce any potential stress. As the hatchlings grow, they will need to be sorted and separated each week according to size. When kept communally,

Young Veiled Chameleons. Photo by Michael Monge.

some hatchlings will eat more vigorously and therefore, will begin to outgrow their cage mates. The smaller chameleons will stress at the constant sight of larger chameleons and eventually go downhill.

Young chameleonids are normally started on small crickets and fruit flies. Generally the length of the chameleon's head will dictate the size of cricket needed throughout the growth process. Most species will start on a one-week-old cricket.

As with the adults, it is very important to use only gut-loaded insects and to dust them with supplement at each feeding. Chameleon hatchlings should be fed daily, however they should never be offered surplus insects to what they will consume daily. When crickets become hungry, they will chew on young chameleons and can create serious physical trauma and even death. It is also vital that hatchlings ingest the supplement coated insects daily for adequate health and growth.

Chapter EIGHT: HEALTH

The damaged eye of this Veiled Chameleon may require veterinary assistance. Photo by Michael Monge.

The key is prompt recognition of ill health or a problem. Like birds, chameleons often hide their ailments and once it becomes very obvious, there is a problem that is well manifested. Often there are more subtle symptoms to watch for.

The vast difference between a captive bred and wild caught chameleon needs to be mentioned here. Wild chameleons are better suited to their now accustomed wild environment. If they are to be considered as an option in captivity, first the potential owner needs to be an experienced chameleon keeper and second, a veterinarian will need to be consulted. Keep in mind, a wild caught chameleon has been subjected to it all – it comes from an environment where it has be exposed to pathogens, it is then stressed, starved, dehydrated and possibly physically hurt before it arrives in captivity. It's also important to remember that the pathogens a chameleon lives with fine in the wild will opportunistically overwhelm the newly compromised immune system and create health problems for the host, but can potentially create an even larger problem to other animals in your care if proper quarantine and cross-contamination procedures are not observed. This is often how viruses are introduced. They will not necessarily harm the host, yet can devastate the entire remainder of a reptile collection. With captive-bred animals, these risks are nearly eliminated.

Aspects to watch for are runny or bloody stools, sunken or swollen eyes, unusual body swellings, loss of balance, loss of appetite, weakness, lethargy, skeletal deformities, skin discolorations or lesions, crusting around any of the orifices, mouth breathing or bubbling from the mouth or nose.

Metabolic Bone Disease

A common ailment and cause of death for chameleons in captivity is MBD. Known as metabolic bone disease or rickets, MBD is caused by an imbalance of phosphorous, calcium and/or Vitamin D_3. Symptoms of MBD are anorexia, loss of coordination in rear legs, spinal kinking, difficulty walking or perching, weak grip, bowed legs, leg tremors, rubbery jawbone or spongy casque. The symptoms of this disease cannot be reversed, but progression of the disease can be stopped with treatment.

Egg Binding

Dystocia or egg binding can be another ailment seen far too often with chameleons in captivity. Most often it is a result of inadequate supplementation or UVB, however other factors than can cause egg binding are inadequate laying site availability, old age, high stress level, other illness that has weakened the female or a physical blockage or deformity. A vet must be consulted immediately for treatment.

Eye Infections

With such unusual visual mechanics, it isn't surprising that eye infections and sensitivity can be one of the more reported ailments. Particles or bacteria can become lodged inside the eye turret and eventually infected or a vitamin A deficiency can create a very similar swelling of the turret. Vitamin A deficiency eye problems are characterized by a lack of response to antibiotic treatment.

Pathogenic Infections

The symptoms of parasitic, bacterial and viral infections are the same, all characterized by weight loss and anorexia, mucous laden, runny and/or bloody stools and sometimes regurgitation of recently eaten food. Any of these pathogens will be fatal if left untreated and require medications with specific indications. Therefore, a veterinarian must be consulted.

Prolapse

Males and females can develop prolapses, which are characterized by a red, fleshy cloacal protrusion. It is the oviduct of the female that prolapses either due to severe nutritional imbalance, constipation or egg binding. A prolapse in males is the hemipene and is either caused by nutritional imbalance also or physical trauma (a twisting or tearing during mating).

There are a few home remedies for this that can be attempted for male prolapses. Either soaking in sugar water or corn starch and water for several hours will sometimes aid in retraction or simply applying firm pressure to the hemipene between the thumb and forefinger will cause the swelling to dissipate and the organ to retract on its own.

Within a few hours the prolapse will begin to dry and will cause the chameleon to go downhill dramatically. A veterinarian should be consulted if you cannot see any improvement within an hour of home treatment.

Renal Failure

Kidney and/or liver damage is caused by severe dehydration, long standing bacterial or viral infection, too much or too little Vitamin D_3 or vitamin A typically. Obviously it is a process of elimination when evaluating husbandry that may point out the specific cause. Like MBD, the effects of renal failure cannot be reversed, but they can be stopped from progressing.

Symptoms sometimes, but not always, include edema (gular swelling) or jaundice (yellowing of the oral tissue). This is often a secondary symptom to a primary ailment and a common cause of death, especially for juveniles and wild caught chameleons. It should be noted that breeding adults suffering from renal failure will pass it on to the hatchlings and as a result, the neonates often live only a few weeks before mysteriously dying often in unexplained numbers.

Respiratory Illness

Characterized by wheezing, mouth breathing, drooling or nasal/mouth bubbling this ailment is easily treated with antibiotics from your veterinarian. It typically develops in an immune compromised animal that has been exposed to another such infected animal or high humidity and low temperatures.

Often medications can create health concern when not administered appropriately and should always be used as indicated by a qualified veterinarian for properly diagnosed ailments. It should also be noted that over use of medications could create an immunity that will invalidate their use when you may really need them or they can cause renal failure in an otherwise healthy animal.

For any health concern, a qualified, reptile experienced veterinarian should be consulted.

THE FUTURE

Photo by Michael Monge.

Chameleons are virtuously harmless creatures, curious and shy and without doubt, unique. Resembling small dinosaurs or dragons, they have inquisitive personalities. At times, they will watch you with interest, until you take note of them. Then their bashful ways will prevail as they quickly turn sideways on a branch or duck behind a leaf, all while keeping at least one eye carefully on you! They are most confident when they think they can't be seen.

For anyone considering a chameleon in captivity, they must understand that very specific needs have to be met. Otherwise a sure death for these gentle creatures will be inevitable. Often by the time a problem manifests, it is too late. Prevention is the key to keeping chameleons in captivity.

Unfortunately, even with protection, chameleons are disapearing in nature as their habitat continues to be destroyed. It's also a greater tragedy for the many chameleons that have died in captivity simply due to poor husbandry and lack of knowledge, and while there has been progress over recent years, there is still more to be discovered . . . far more. I seem to have a good talent, primarily due to my honest passion for these gentle spirits, for keeping chameleons in captivity, but I still believe it can be better. For me, that's a daily passion and it's my wish to perfect and strengthen life for chameleons in captivity along with other keepers who feel as I do.

For now, this book is meant as a start to husbandry for any chameleon enthusiast. I made strides with these creatures that at one time were described as difficult and impossible in captivity. When I purchased my first chameleon, it was my first reptile and the shop owner strongly advised against my purchase of it. Over a decade ago, I took that responsibility seriously. I have personally captive produced eighteen different species and for many of them several generations. Success to keeping and reproducing chameleons in captivity can and will be strengthened. If it's your decision to own a chameleon as a pet, learn all you can and together we will all add to an even higher increase in success and longevity for the old world chameleon in captivity!

Thank you.

CONNIE DORVAL

Founder,
Arboreal Exotics

INDIVIDUAL SPECIES ACCOUNTS: The Veiled Chameleon, the Panther Chameleon, and Jackson's Chameleon

The specifics for keeping a chameleon in captivity, in terms of temperature, humidity and sometimes nutrition, does differ with each individual species. Not only does the fact that some species come from different locales make the difference, however even within the same locale each species has adopted life at a different range, which can play a factor in its captive care.

An adult male Veiled Chameleon. Photo by Bill Love.

Naturally it's easy to guess that of the many different species of chameleon, there is a range of level among the species when it comes to captive husbandry and success. While I have personally kept and reproduced many different species in captive conditions, I find it interesting to note that sometimes species previously listed as beginner chameleons are not so and some that are listed as difficult, can be easier to maintain than expected.

The horned Jackson's Chameleon was once the most commonly available species in the pet trade. Photo by Bob Ashley.

For the true novice, in my opinion and experience, I always recommend one of two species to begin with if you are inexperienced with keeping a chameleon as a pet. They are the veiled chameleon (*C. calyptratus*) and the panther chameleon (*F. pardalis*). Both of these species seem to have a range of forgiveness in the husbandry required to keep them successfully that many chameleon species do not share.

The Panther Chameleon
Furcifer pardalis

A spectacular male Panther Chameleon from the Ambanja area of Madagascar. Photo by Bill Love.

Panther Chameleons are found along the northern and northeastern coast of Madagascar. They were typically found in primary rainforest but are one of the species that has benefited greatly from man's interference in the environment. Banana and coffee plantations have attracted insect life and the chameleons have spread into these areas and are found in large numbers, basking in the trees and feeding on the insects there.

While *F. pardalis* seems to like basking, they appear to enjoy the heat in limited doses. Often a panther chameleon in captivity will routinely begin its day basking in a favorite spot and will by mid-morning to afternoon wander away to a cooler section of the enclosure, sometimes returning for a small dose of heat later in the day. This is unlike *C. calyptratus* that will simply stay put beneath the basking site for the entire day.

F. pardalis come from a coastal forested region. It is reported that they require high humidity in captivity, however from experience I do

Stress coloration is obvious in the specimen on the right. Photo by Michael Monge.

not agree. Low to moderate humidity levels work well and can be accomplished through hand misting. Panther chameleons are prone to fungal infections when kept at high humidity levels, particularly in combination with temperatures that are too high or too low consistently. A basking site of 85° F to 90° F is ideal and the option of a lower temperature area away from this heat is quite necessary with this species. As with all other species, a night drop of about 10 degrees is also important. Young panther chameleons cannot tolerate high temperatures for any length of time. It's best for the first four months to keep young *F. pardalis* between 75° F and 80° F.

Sexing adult panther chameleons is quite easy. Males are typically twice the size of females and display the famous beautiful coloration that panthers are noted for. Males also have an obvious hemipenal swelling. Females are smaller and always a range of brown to orange in color. As hatchlings, *F. pardalis* can be sexed with experience. Males do exhibit a wider taper in the tail by the cloaca than the females, even upon hatching. With juveniles, color can never be an accurate sexing means even though as adults there is a notable difference in color and markings.

Male *F. pardalis* seem to have an incredible range of color and markings that appear representative of the specific locale they are

A green Panther Chameleon from Diego Suarez, Madagascar. Photo by Bill Love.

from within Madagascar.

Females also exhibit markings that slightly differ from one another depending on locale, however it is far more difficult to assess upon observation. It has been noted on many occasions that crossing panther chameleons from two different locales (which will create hybrid coloration) will produce mules or sterile animals. I do believe there is truth to this theory, though I suspect it doesn't appear prominently until the second generation.

Males will show aggression toward one another and as a rule should be kept singly. Females, however, will tolerate communal cohabitation if the enclosure allows in terms of space.

One last note in regard to *F. pardalis* is nutritional. Panther chameleons seem to require higher doses of vitamin A than most other chameleon species in captivity. For this reason, it is important that a vitamin supplement with this in mind be used regularly in conjunction with the recommended calcium/D3 supplement.

The Veiled Chameleon
Chameleo calyptratus

The Veiled Chameleon is found along the coastline of Yemen and southern Saudi Arabia. There are two subspecies of Veiled Chamelons currently recognized by taxonomists. *Chameleo calyptratus calyptratus* is the larger subspecies that is familiar to the hobby. *C. c. calcarifer* is a smaller chameleon with a smaller casque. It is not being kept in captivity today.

Photo by Bob Ashley.

This sun-loving chameleon can be found from desert to mountainous regions and while it has a reputation for enjoying the heat, there have been stories of this chameleon being found in regions of frost at odd times.

C. calyptratus can tolerate temperatures up to and even just beyond 100° F and down to as low as 50° F. However, the ideal basking temperature for them is 85° F to 90° F with a slight gradient within the enclosure. At night all heat and light sources must shut down to allow the chameleon to cool. A 10 degree drop at night is ideal. Keep in mind that young veiled chameleons cannot tolerate the same high basking temperatures as the adults. Until four months of age, young veiled chameleons should be kept at a high of 82° F and less if

An adult female Veiled Chameleon. Photo by Bill Love.

a temperature gradient is not possible within their enclosure.

C. calyptratus can tolerate high humidity, but do not seem to require it in captivity. A daily offering of water is required via spraying and/or drip system.

This is one of the very few species that will learn to enjoy vegetation as part of their diet. However, vegetation can only make up an addition to their diet. Insects must stay as the main staple. Each individual veiled chameleon appears to have its own individual taste, therefore the keeper may have to experiment with their particular animal. Plants of interest are *Ficus benjamina*, hibiscus, *Pothos*, dandelion, and even sunflowers. Always be sure that plants are non-toxic and free of insecticides. Vegetables enjoyed can be green beans, snow peas, broccoli, romaine lettuce, and carrots. Even fruits such as apples, oranges, strawberries, banana, and pears are relished. These mixed "salads" should be finely grated.

Sexing *C. calyptratus* is very easy and can be done right from hatching. Males have a small tarsal spur at the back of their hind feet. Females do not. At maturity, males also have larger casques than females and more color. Males display ranges of blue, green,

A healthy and alert juvenile Veiled Chameleon. Photo by Michael Monge.

orange, yellow and/or brown. Females are typically all green with small patches of tan and orange.

It should also be noted that while veiled chameleons learn to tolerate handling well, they are considered one of the most aggressive chameleon species and should be housed singly and under observation even when introduced for breeding.

Jackson's Chameleons
Chameleo jacksonii

A healthy adult male Jackson's Chameleon. Photo by Bill Love.

At one time, Jackson's chameleons were a staple in the pet trade for many years. Their unusual triceratops appearance made them one of the most sought after reptiles in the hobby when they were imported from Africa. However, very few people seemed to do well with this particular species long term.

Of the many species I have reproduced over and over successfully (and the Jackson's were one of them), I would consider this species to be one of the more tempermental and advise their captive consideration be for experienced chameleon keepers only.

C. jacksonii are found in the montane regions of Tanzania and Kenya in high rainforest elevations. They have also been introduced

An adult female Jackson's Chameleon. Photo by Bill Love.

and thrive on some islands of Hawaii. There are three recognized sub-species: *C. jacksonii*, *C. jacksonii xantholophus*, *C. jacksonii merumontanus*.

C. jacksonii is wide ranging on the southern and western slopes of Mount Kenya.

C. j. xantholophus is the largest form found on the eastern and southern sides of Mount Kenya.

C. j. merumontanus is the dwarf form found from Mount Meru to Tanzania.

As with all chameleon species, the larger the enclosure the better. The most common problem with Jackson's in captivity is their susceptibility to low-grade stress. Since they are by nature one of the more easy going and gentle chameleons, keepers often do not see any sign of ill husbandry until it has overwhelmed the chameleon and it's often too late. One of the most common recounts of Jackson keepers is that they seem to do well for approximately six to eight months and then go down hill.

Jackson's need a well-planted enclosure with optimal ventilation.

A female Jackson's Chameleon. Photo by Bill Love.

Screened enclosures are the best for this species. Humidity should be kept over 65%. Ideally, Jackson's prefer spraying two to three times daily and a drip system. This species vitally needs good hydration.

Another common mistake keepers make with this species is temperature. Unlike most other chameleon species in captivity, Jackson's have to have access to cool daytime temps and a basking site that dramatically range in temperature. Most species of chameleon in captivity do need a gradient of about ten degrees or so (many can even handle constant ambient temps), however *C. jacksonii* require a cool daytime backdrop temperature of 70° to 75° F with a basking sight of 85° F. Constant ambient temps will cause low-grade stress and typically lead to death in less than a year in captivity. Over heating this species will also cause death, particularly very quickly in neonates.

Jackson's are very easy to sex. Males have three horns approximately ½ to 1" long and a wider tail base. The females are lacking these horns or only have very small nubs. The babies can typically be accurately sexed at three to four months of age when young males start developing noticeable horns.

Jackson's are one of the chameleon species that often becomes bored with the same food item (most chameleons should be offered variety any way). For this reason, it's quite important to introduce variety weekly. As with most live bearing and/or montane chameleon species, Jackson's fair better on lower doses of artificial

A large enclosure that houses a trio of Jackson's Chameleons. Photo by Bob Ashley.

supplementation. While some species require more vitamins such as the Panther for example, this species requires less. I did well supplementing with plain calcium twice a week, calcium with D3 two to three times weekly and a vitamin supplement once or twice a month. Of course, it's still very important to gut load insects as well.

Breeding

Jackson's are ovoviviparous which means they are a live bearing species. When a pair is introduced, if the female maintains relaxed coloration and posture she is likely receptive. The male will approach and she will allow him to mount if still interested. Typically females will only allow copulation when ovulating and receptive to producing young.

If the female is not interested, she will darken in color, gape at the male and likely rock back and forth. If this occurs she should be removed and introduced again two weeks later.

Gestation for the Jackson chameleon is about six to nine months. This live bearing species, depending on sub-species, will produce anywhere from ten to fifty babies at one time. Each baby is encased

A baby Jackson's Chameleon. Photo by Bill Love.

in a membrane sack and at birth is dropped from the female cloaca to the ground. The newborn Jackson should begin to struggle and emerge from the sack with five to ten minutes of being dropped. If the neonate does not move within the sack, pick it up and drop it on the enclosure floor with a firm thump. This will most often stimulate the neonate to struggle out. I don't recommend helping the neonate out of the sack. This process develops strength. If a neonate cannot emerge, it likely won't thrive well long term even if you help it out. A solid thud should stimulate them to start living on their own.

Babies should be removed and placed in their own enclosure within an hour or two of birth. Live bearing females usually will not eat their young after birth, but if the babies are not removed the female may eventually start to eat them.
The babies should be kept at slightly cooler temps than the adults. Typically 70° to 76° F works well. Over heating will rapidly kill the neonates.

Jackson's are sexually mature at about ten months of age.

Pygmy Chameleons

A Pygmy Leaf Chameleon, *Rhampholeon brevicauda*. Photo by Michael Monge.

The two genera of chameleons, *Brookesia* and *Rhampholeon* are referred to as pygmy, leaf or stump-tailed chameleons. These chameleons are considered independent of true chameleon genera's (*Bradypdion*, *Calumma*, *Chamaeleo* and *Furcifer*).

Brookesia are found in Madagascar. *Rhampholeon* are found within Africa.

Pygmy chameleons are forest-dwelling, found mostly in moist conditions such as rainforest or humid evergreen forests. They inhabit the lowest forest vegetation and even hide within leaf litter usually only a few inches at most above the ground soil.

The appearance of these tiny chameleons is unlike any of the other genera. Pygmy chameleons strongly resemble fallen leaves and twigs with drab coloration similar to that found on the forest floor.

Unlike most other chameleon species whose tail is often the length of their head and body or longer, pygmy chameleons have tails that are shorter than the length of the head and body. The also have more rigid, and frail stick-like legs and are not nearly as agile at movement as the other genera species would be.

Keeping pygmy chameleons in captivity has been difficult for many keepers. Also some species seem to fair better than others in a captive environment. I personally have done well with a few different species and managed to reproduce them over the years. As tiny as the babies are, I wouldn't consider them problematic at all. (I would consider *C. jacksonii*, *C. hoehnelii* or *C. montium* to be more difficult.) In fact once the adults are acclimated, captive pygmies seem to fair well in my opinion as long as their specified husbandry needs are met.

These species especially need to feel invisible. It's important to create a vivarium that looks like a forest floor. Using an open aquarium or plastic container line the floor with at least two inches of plain soil (it works better if a little sand and natural litter is mixed in to give more texture). Then add a few sturdy rocks, dead leaves, twigs, etc. A plant or two (artificial or live) can be added along the soil floor. Remember these chameleons don't like to travel high. They prefer to travel *through* bunched, messy and decaying forest strata.

With observation, it doesn't take long to realize pygmy chameleons do not like a lot of light. Consequently, they don't like heat either.

Under lights these chameleons will often squint or close their eyes. They prefer cooler ambient temperatures between 70° to 75° F daytime and only filtered light. Often I found they preferred ambient room light to any artificial sources. I always had the best success using a low watt incandescent plant grow bulb mounted one to two feet away. I would time the bulb to come on in the morning and go out by lunch.

Pygmy chameleons need a moist environment, but not wet. They seem to thrive on two to three sprayings a day.

Pygmy chameleons will eat small crickets (no larger than the length of their head) and fruit flies. I have also always introduced springtails and wood lice into the soil and offered very small silk worms. The crickets and fruit flies are always supplemented as mentioned previously in this book for other chameleon genera.

An adult and juvenile Pygmy Leaf Chameleon, *Rhampholeon brevicauda*. Animals courtesy of Eric Haug. Photo by Bill Love.

I have successfully kept small groups together with one male pygmy to two or three females. However, it's important to have enough space for each individual to establish a personal perching site. Pygmy chameleons especially seem to chose a spot within the vivarium and remain there most of the time and will get upset at a cage mate when that favorite site is invaded.

Males are typically smaller than females and can be noted by their obvious hemipenal swelling once mature. Males also tend to have slightly longer tails than the females.

I almost never saw copulation, though not surprising considering the high secretive nature of these chameleons, however I could nearly always recognize a gravid female by her increasing size and appetite. Consequently I always knew when to look for eggs because the female would be noticeably thinner.

I have successfully incubated this species in both vermiculite and soil. Brookesia usually hatch in two to four months. Rhampholeon usually take a little longer hatching in three to six months. I have found lower room temps of about 68° to 72° F best to incubate the eggs. In fact, I've had eggs hatch right in the vivaria with the adults whom did not seem inclined to eat the young.

Young pygmy chameleons thrive on the same regime as the adults with appropriate sized insects.

PHOTO GALLERY

A spectacular male Panther Chameleon. Photo by Michael Monge.

The famous "Pink Panther" *F. pardalis* from Ankaremy Be, Madagascar. Photo by Bill Love.

A male Panther Chameleon from Ambanja, Madagascar enjoying a rain shower. Photo by Bill Love.

A beautiful orange and peach-colored male Panther Chameleon. Photo by Tyler Stewart.

A male Ambanja Blue Panther Chameleon. Photo by Bill Love.

A green, red, and blue Panther Chameleon. Photo by Michael Monge.

A male Panther Chameleon from Antsiranana, Madagascar. Photo by Bill Love.

A gravid female Panther Chameleon. Photo by Tyler Stewart.

An adult male Veiled Chameleon with a juvenile along for the ride. Photo by Bill Love.

An adult female Veiled Chameleon. Photo by Bill Love.

An adult male Jackson's Chameleon, *Chamaeleo jacksonii*. Photo by Bill Love.

An adult male Chameleon, *Chamaeleo deremensis*. Photo by Michael Monge.

An adult male Side-striped Chameleon, *Chamaeleo rudis*, from Tanzania. Photo by Michael Monge.

An adult female Side-striped Chameleon, *Chamaeleo rudis*, from Tanzania. Photo by Michael Monge.

An excited Carpet Chameleon, *Chamaeleo lateralis*. Photo by Michael Monge.

The Flap-necked Chameleon, *Chamaeleo dilepis*. Photo by Bill Love.

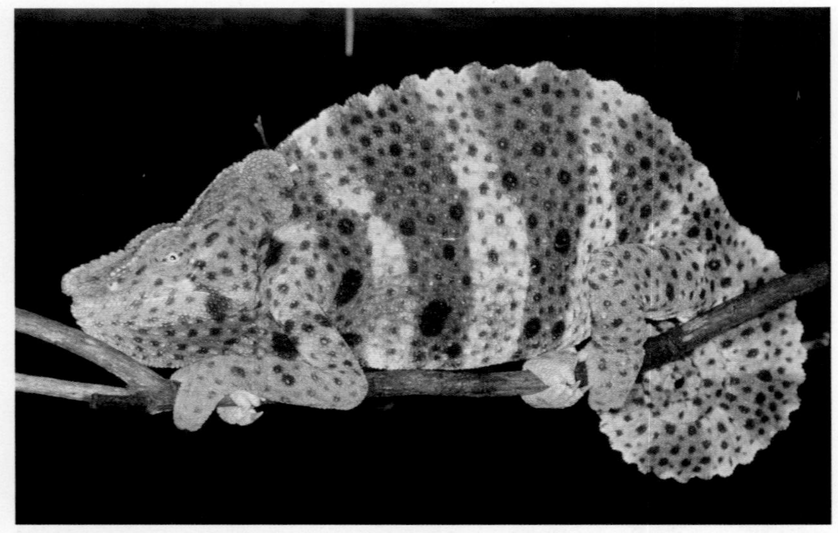

Meller's Chameleon, *Chamaeleo melleri*. Photo by Bill Love.

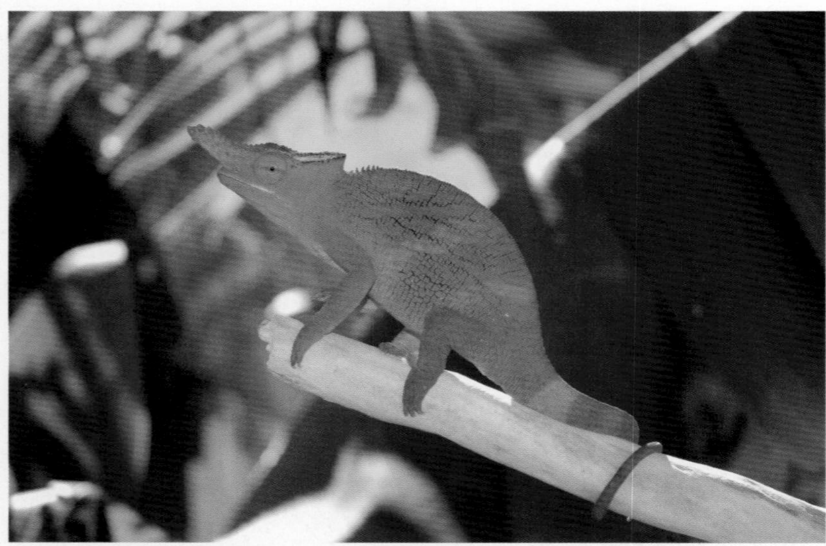

An adult male Fischer's Chameleon, *Chamaeleo fischeri*. Photo by Micheal Monge.

The large Oustalet's Chameleon, *Chamaeleo oustaleti*, from the thorny scrubland of south-central Madagascar. Photo by Bill Love.

An impressive adult male Parson's Chameleon, *Chamaeleo parsoni*. Photo by Bill Love.

SUGGESTED READING

Davison, L.J. 1997. Chameleons: Their Care and Breeding. Hancock House Publishers Ltd., Surrey, British Columbia.

de Vosjoli, P. and G. Ferguson. 1995. Care and Breeding of Chameleons. Advanced Vivarium Systems, Lakeside, California.

Martin, J. 1992. Masters of Disguise (A Natural History of Chameleons). Facts On File, Inc., New York.

Necas, P. 2004. Chameleons: Nature's Hidden Jewels. Edition Chimaira / Serpents Tale.